YOUNG WOMEN'S EDITION

MUSIC THEATRE INTERNATIONAL'S

BROADWAY *junior* SONGBOOK

AUDIO ACCESS INCLUDED
Recorded Performances and Accompaniments Online

To access companion recorded performances
and accompaniments online, visit:
www.halleonard.com/mylibrary

Enter Code
6489-4316-8432-8328

ISBN 978-0-634-09519-1

HAL•LEONARD®

Visit Hal Leonard Online at
www.halleonard.com

Contact us:
Hal Leonard
7777 West Bluemound Road
Milwaukee, WI 53213
Email: info@halleonard.com

In Europe, contact:
Hal Leonard Europe Limited
42 Wigmore Street
Marylebone, London, W1U 2RN
Email: info@halleonardeurope.com

In Australia, contact:
Hal Leonard Australia Pty. Ltd.
4 Lentara Court
Cheltenham, Victoria, 3192 Australia
Email: info@halleonard.com.au

These solo selections for young singers are
drawn from the revolutionary *Broadway Junior
Collection*, which presents author-approved,
condensed versions of classic musicals. Keys
have been adjusted for typical young voices,
and the songs have been slightly edited from the
original show versions. Young singers will surely
benefit from hearing a voice their own age on the
audio. The recorded orchestrated accompaniments
will inspire the feeling of a true performance.

Find out more about
The Broadway Junior Collection **by visiting:**
www.halleonard.com/broadwayjunior

MAYBE
from the Musical Production *Annie*

Lyric by Martin Charnin
Music by Charles Strouse

hid - den by a hill, she's sit - tin' play - in' pi -

a - no, he's sit - tin' pay - in' a bill!

Bet - cha they're young. Bet - cha they're smart. Bet they col - lect___ things like

ash - trays and art!___ Bet - cha they're good.___ Why shouldn't they be?___

Their one mis-take was giv-in' up me!___ So,

may - be now it's time, and may - be when I wake,

they'll be there, call - in' me "Ba - by," may -

a tempo

be.

Bet-cha he reads. Bet-cha she sews. May-be she's made— me a

clos-et of clothes!— May-be they're strict,— as straight as a line.—

Don't real-ly care, as long as they're mine!— So,

may - be now this prayer's the last one of its kind:

won't you please come get your "Ba - by,"

may - be?

TOMORROW
from the Musical Production *Annie*

Lyric by Martin Charnin
Music by Charles Strouse

sor - row, ___ 'til there's none! When I'm stuck_ with a

day that's gray and lone - ly, I just stick_ out my chin and grin and

say, "Oh, the sun -'ll come out___ to - mor - row,

so ya got - ta hang on 'til to - mor-row, come what may." To -

11

DAY BY DAY
from the Musical *Godspell*

Words and Music by
Stephen Schwartz

Easy waltz feel (♩ = 98)

Day by day, day by day,

Oh, dear Lord three things I pray:

to see thee more clear - ly, love thee more dear - ly,

Light rock feel (♩ = 136)

fol-low thee more near - ly, day by day.

Day by day, _____ day by day, _____ Oh, _____ dear

Lord three things I pray: _____ to see thee more clear - ly,

love thee more dear - ly, fol-low thee more near - ly, _____ day by day. _____

More forceful

Day by day, _____ day by day, _____

8vb

16

Oh, dear Lord three things I pray: to see thee more clear - ly, love thee more dear - ly, fol-low thee more near - ly, day by day.

A little harder still

(opt. claps)

Day by day, day by day,

ADELAIDE'S LAMENT
from *Guys and Dolls*

By Frank Loesser

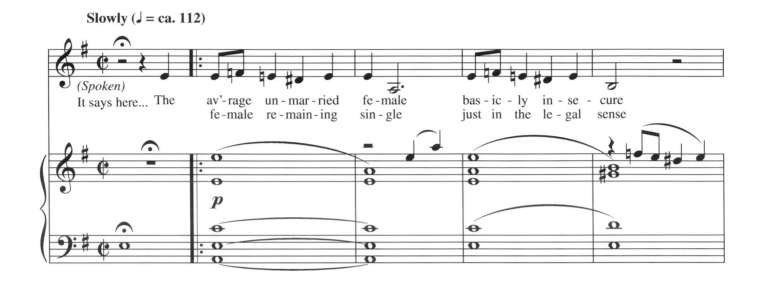

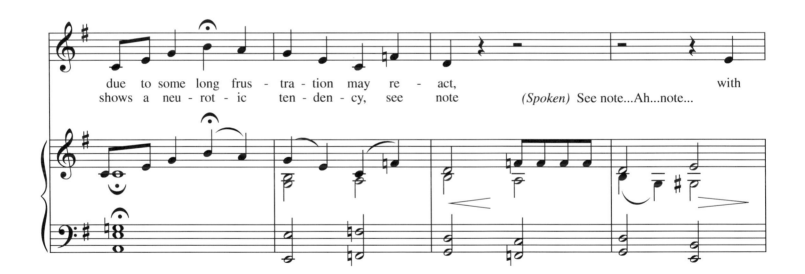

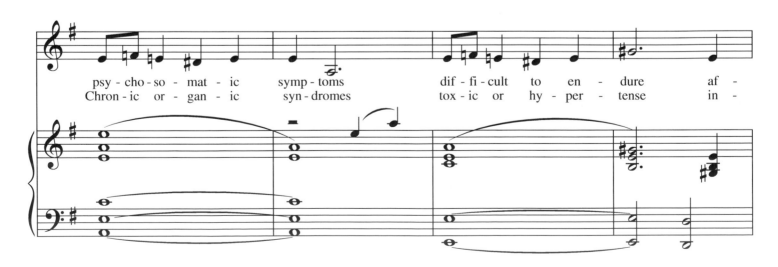

church bells chime,____ the com - part - ment is air con - di - tioned____ and the

mood sub - lime.____ Then they get off a Sa - ra - to - ga____ for the

four - teenth time,____ a per - son can de - vel - op La

grippe, (Hm!) La grippe, La post - na - sal drip, with the

whee - zes and the snee - zes and a si - nus that's real - ly a pip! From a

lack of com - mu - ni - ty pro - per - ty____ and a feel - ing she's get - ting too old, A

per - son can de - vel - op a bad bad

cold.____

IF I WERE A BELL
from *Guys and Dolls*

By Frank Loesser

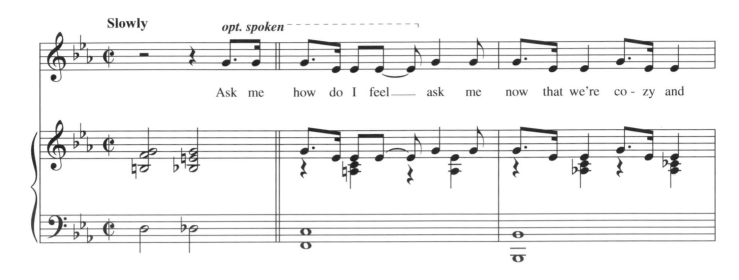

TILL THERE WAS YOU
from Meredith Willson's *The Music Man*

By Meredith Willson

dawn and dew. There was love all a-

round, but I nev - er heard it sing - ing. No, I

nev - er heard it at all, till there was you.

espr. molto

GOODNIGHT, MY SOMEONE

from Meredith Willson's *The Music Man*

By Meredith Willson

INTERPLANET JANET

from *Schoolhouse Rock Live!*

Words and Music by
Lynn Ahrens

some-where out in space there's an - oth-er shin - ing face that

you might see some night up in the sky wav-ing "Hi!"__

In - ter - plan - et Jan - et, she's a gal - ax - y girl, a so - lar sys-tem Ms from a

fu - ture world.__ She trav-els like a rock - et with her com - et team,__ and there's

never been a plan-et Jan-et has-n't seen. No, there's nev-er been a plan-et Jan-et

has-n't seen.____ She's been to the sun, it's a lot of fun! It's a

hot spot, it's a gas.____ Hy-dro-gen and he-li-um____ in a

big, bright, glow-ing mass.____ It's a star,____ it's a star,____ so

Jan-et got an au-to-graph!___ Uh, huh!___ Mer-cu-ry was near the sun so

Jan-et stopped by,___ but the mer-cu-ry on Mer-cu-ry was much to high,___ so

Jan-et split for Ve-nus, but on Ve-nus she found___ she could-n't see a thing for all the

clouds a-round.___ Earth looked ex-cit-ing, kind of green and in-vit-ing, so

Jan - et thought she'd give it a go.___ But the crea-tures on that plan - et looked so

ver - y weird to Jan - et, she did - n't e - ven dare to say "Hel - lo." It's a bird!

___ It's a plane!___ Why, it must be a U. F. O.!___

___ But it was In - ter - plan - et Jan - et she's a gal - ax - y girl,___ a

ra-nus is built on a fun-ny tilt,___ and Nep-tune is___ its twin.___ And

Plu-to, lit-tle Plu-to, is the far-thest plan-et from our sun.___ Some___

fu-ture as-tro-naut___ may find out that what she thought___ a

shoot-ing star___ in-stead turned out to be___